T0199181

CHOSEN

My Heart to Heart Journey to Purpose

Daryl Johnson

To order additional copies of this book, contact:
Xlibris
1-888-795-4274
www.Xlibris.com
Orders@Xlibris.com

Scripture quotations marked KJV are from the Holy Bible, King James Version (Authorized Version). First published in 1611. Quoted from the KJV Classic Reference Bible, Copyright © 1983 by The Zondervan Corporation.

ISBN: 978-1-7960-9412-1 (sc)
ISBN: 978-1-7960-9411-4 (hc)
ISBN: 978-1-7960-9410-7 (e)

Print information available on the last page

Rev. date: 05/29/2020

CHOSEN

Chosen

My Heart-to-Heart Journey to Purpose

Daryl Johnson

This book is dedicated to God, my Father, Jesus Christ, my Lord and Savior, and the Holy Spirit. Thank you for your blessings and mercies in carrying me to and through my life's arduous journey that I was destined to experience. Thank you for New Life, A New Heart for A New Start.

To my family, relatives, friends, classmates, teammates, church family, and, lastly, the Houston Methodist Hospital transplant/cardiovascular units (everyone), thank you. Thank you for your prayers, support, and service. Your blessings and kindness will never be forgotten.

To the spirit of my donor and the giving of his family, may God forever bless and thank you for your gift.

Contents

FOREWORD

My name is Daryl Johnson (Doc or Dr. J to most who know me).

In my writing and your reading of this book, you will receive an insight into my life. Identified will be my ambitions, pitfalls, triumphs, failures, and loves. As you read *Chosen*, you will experience the many twists and turns, highs and lows, and ups and downs to this fabulous and sometimes unbelievable journey of my life. *I am chosen*. I hope you will enjoy my "heart-to-heart journey to my purpose."

Over the past four years, my life has taken many turns. I was a successful business owner and entrepreneur helping the less fortunate, a healthy Pro Am basketball player (playing for thirty-five-plus years). Allow me to take you back in time for a moment where this unimaginable journey began.

Chosen

I was attending church service one Sunday, and the sermon was about Job. While I was listening to my pastor, my mind drifted to a point where I wondered if I could be like Job, losing all his earthly possessions and still remaining a devoted servant of and to God. Well, little did I know I was about to be tested to the uttermost within a week. You see, sometimes in life, God will set you up when His will has to be done and you're operating at your own time and pace. The pastor closed his sermon by requesting us to attend service during the week and not just be Sunday worshippers. He expressed that we needed the Word during the week for strength building and survival from Satan and his temptations.

I just kind of said to myself, *He's not really talking to me. I've been playing basketball on this night for over thirty-five years.* For many of you who know me, you know that basketball was and is my love. It was the one thing on the natural scale that I had always been in sync with. I was playing in the National Pro Am basketball league, which is one level shy of playing in the NBA. Our team was considered one of the nation's best playing teams, defeating some pro teams and winning multiple team championships. I was coming to the end of my career and had started to slow down to allow the younger players to play more.

Suddenly, I began to play great. My teammates and opponents began to see the change.

They marveled and said, "Daryl, you've found the fountain of youth."

I was flattered because I had recognized the change too. Life, I thought, had become great again!.

It had become time for my annual physical. I took the atomic physical, which is toughest they administered, and passed with great success.

Now it was on to Dallas to play in the Texas Pro Am Championships, where we encountered many obstacles. We were tested in all phases from the schedule, acquiring injuries and mixed-up hotel arrangements. Perplexed but determined to win, we played and won our way to the championship game.

In that game, we were the underdogs. The opposing team jumped out to a large lead, and my teammates, who were younger, began to lose their composure, and their confidence was altered. However, being the captain, I always had this saying: "Don't worry about a thing."

Sometimes in life, you will find yourself at a disadvantage and have to dig deep to overcome insurmountable obstacles. We reached down, reached back, found some of that "old magic," and did what veterans do. By the time the third quarter was beginning, we had closed the gap to ten points. From there, we went on to win the championship—110 to 101. Afterward, we celebrated our hard-earned victory. Later that night, we arrived in Houston safely to get ready for our normal jobs.

Stricken

The next morning, I sat on the sofa, preparing for the day, and suddenly, I began to experience a pain like I had never felt before from head to toe. I thought maybe I had gotten food poisoning. I was talking to a friend on the phone, describing the pain, and I was instructed to call 911. I crawled to unlock the door and made the call. When the paramedics arrived, they began to administer treatment while talking among themselves. I knew then that something was wrong. They immediately secured me and took me to emergency. After many hours and tests, I was informed that my kidneys were failing.

Shock

Well, much to my chagrin, I said, "I don't have a kidney problem." I told them to double-check because of my recent physical results. I conveyed, "I shouldn't be having any of those kinds of symptoms."

They said, "Mr. Johnson, we don't have to. There's a blood clot at the entrance of your kidney, causing them to fail. Tests indicate your heart is being severely affected, causing its rhythm to go awry."

In addition, the tests showed that the blockage of my kidneys was causing my heart rate to climb to 350 plus. I wasn't receiving any blood flow. I realized, *That ain't good.* I was later told my heart should have blown up (first miracle). I received several blood-clot–dissolving treatments to remove them. After four days of testing, the test revealed that more clots had developed in my heart, one in the front and another in the rear.

The clots had already passed through my brain, and (second miracle) to make matters worse, I had induced and survived a medical overdose of morphine from the self-medication device and survived. Several attempts were made to dissolve them, but it wasn't to be. A medical ablation was scheduled, and I was prepped for surgery. The surgical procedure was performed. However, while they were doing so, more blood clots were discovered at the back of my heart. If that wasn't enough, additional test results indicated that the surgical ablation couldn't be performed because of the density of my blood. I began to wonder, *What else, God?*

It took five months to get the blood density correct, and during that time, I caught the shingles and contracted asthma. It took more than two months to clear up the shingles; the normal incubation time is thirty days. Along with it all, I still had the asthma, which resulted in congestive heart failure. It seemed my well-being was in a constant state of peril.

Three months passed, and we received the approval for surgery. Finally, the moment for surgery arrived. I was on the surgical table, receiving sedation with anesthesia, and suddenly, the tech rushed in, yelling to stop. He told the surgeon if they continued, I would surely bleed to death because my blood was too thin. The surgery was postponed, disappointment and disgust set in, and my situation was getting worse.

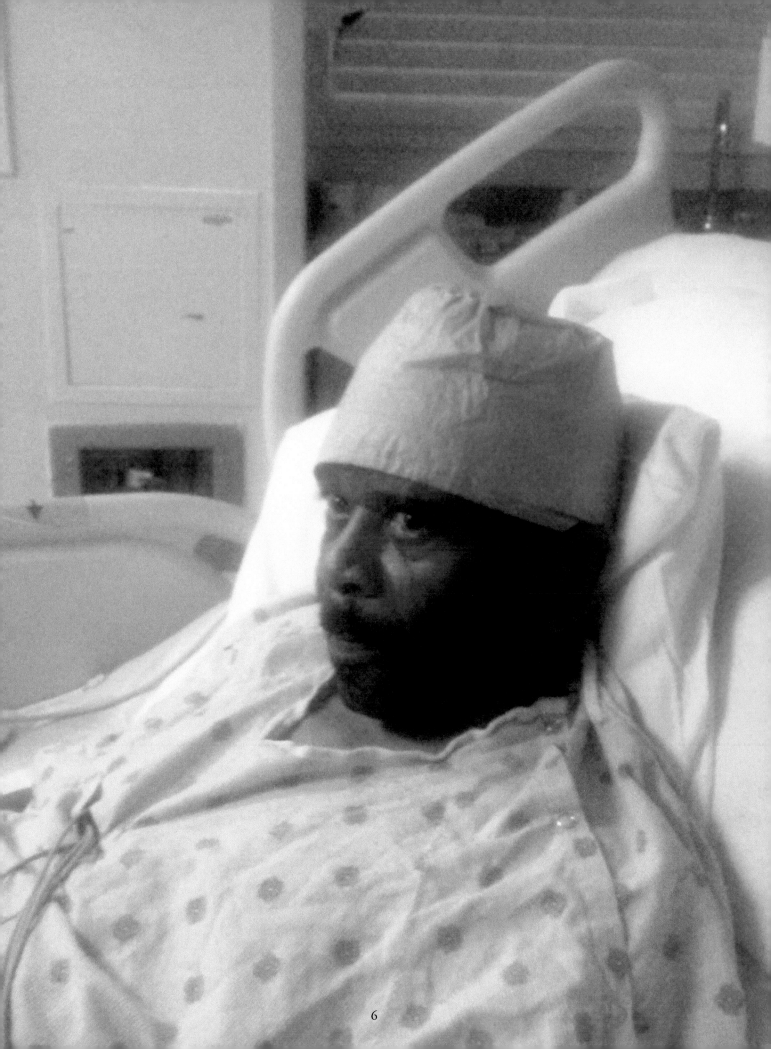

Three long months passed, and I was set up for surgical consultation. The doctor had come, highly acclaimed, with a great bedside manner. He was precise and direct in his explanation of the procedure to take place. It was going to be a new procedure; however, it was the best thing to do considering my condition.

After making me feel comfortable, he then closed with a bombshell, saying, "Daryl, I'll be honest with you. There's a chance you could die."

On the way home, I began to think, *How could this happen to me?* I then realized I had no choice. The situation was getting worse. I talked with my family, and my decision was made to proceed.

Surgery

I was attached to life-support machines for the open heart surgery. They removed my heart to take out the front- and rear-end blood clots. My heart was really weak. It was then decided for me to have a front-end ablation to assist my heart in keeping a consistent rhythm.

During recovery, something went wrong. It was discovered that I had developed a hole in my windpipe going to my lungs. It had developed from the previous surgery, and it caused me to cough blood and fluid for two days. I was unable to have surgery to correct this newfound issue. My body had been severely weakened from the two previous surgeries.

On the third day, they operated on my windpipe. I was in recovery for the next two days. A horrendous cough had developed, and the doctors couldn't stop it. I coughed all day and night long. Medication was seemingly not the answer. Finally, on the fifth day, the surgeon came into my room and said I needed to have emergency surgery to live. My lungs had collapsed and were filling up with fluid. I began to develop an uneasiness in my spirit, all the while trusting in God.

One day the specialists had created an atmosphere of panic. I was losing pressure, and my support needs became more eminent as time went on. My needs for an electro heart treatment had to be done immediately. The electric heart treatments were not given twice but three times, surpassing the normal amount of requirements.

My heart began to beat at an acceptable rate, but the emergency surgery on my lungs was still required. My lungs were collapsing, and needless to say, I became frustrated and ready to give up. I asked God, *Why?* Had I been so terrible in my past that I deserved this as a punishment?

God's response was "I chose you. This is not about you, Daryl Johnson, but you will learn a great deal. It will be for the manifestation to others that they may recognize my greatness, power, and mercy." He comforted me and gave me a battle cry in the form of Psalms 23:4—"Yea, though I walk through the valley of the shadow of death, I will fear no evil, for Thou art with me. Thy rod and Thy staff, they comforted me."

My faith showed up. I gathered my thoughts and prayed. *Father, you've been with me on the previous surgeries, and now it's time to take another ride.*

The surgery took place at 5:00 a.m. on Saturday, and I didn't awaken until Sunday evening at 6:00 pm. (fourth, fifth, and sixth miracles). The seventh miracle was that I had had four major surgeries in six days. As I awakened in recovery and tried moving, I discovered there were three large holes in my back attached to three large garden-size hoses. The holes were receptacles for blood and fluid draining from my lungs. The pain was horrific, but the surgery was a success. The news went out among the hospital employees, and they came to see from all over the hospital.

One doctor broke down in tears, and another said, "You must know someone."

I responded, "Yes I do."

I wasn't out of the woods yet. The next week, my ablation had to be redone. The following week, three more electric shocks were administered. They were really trying to keep me alive. I wasn't getting any better. The blood clots were gone, but I couldn't seem to get over the hump. I was just holding on. My heart rhythm was irregular, and my blood wasn't clotting correctly. To top it all off, I couldn't sleep.

One day I was in so much pain, I asked the doctors if there was something they could do, and they said no. Everything had already been done. My nurses were crying because they couldn't provide any resources to help ease my pain. I couldn't do anything but scream.

I sat up in bed, and out of my mouth came "Jesus." God heard my cry!

From that moment on, I began to improve, and now I'm a case study. *Won't he do it?*

The doctors marveled when coming by my room to visit. Their comments were that they had to come and see "the miracle patient." One doctor was so amazed that while talking to me, she had forgotten her duties.

She even went on to say as she cried, "I'm going to talk with my children and tell them I've seen and talked to a miracle."

Job 19:25 states, "I know my redeemer lives." God lets you know there is nothing impossible for Him. He is still on the throne and cannot be defeated.

Moving On

After three months, I finally got out of the hospital and began the long road to recovery. There were many long days and sleepless nights. It instilled doubt of my healing. The doctors explained that the symptoms were normal and my need to get adjusted. The medicine was horrible, creating a sense of despair. However, I pressed on, continuing the recovery process appropriately and expectantly.

I resumed working out, and of course, that included basketball. I shot the basketball unexpectedly well, and I was pleased with my progress. Life was looking up. I went for my regular monthly checkups, and the doctors were pleased. On one occasion, the preliminary assessment of my tests had been completed. Things seemed satisfactory to the doctors, and I awaited the completed results.

Several days passed, and I had not received the results. So I called the doctor's office. After I had identified myself, the nurse dropped the phone and started to scream for the doctor. She found him.

His first point of conversation was "Mr. Johnson, I need you to go to the emergency room immediately. The staff will be waiting and will explain upon your arrival."

I wasn't satisfied, and I insisted that he tell me. I inquired, "What's wrong, Doctor?"

He said, "Mr. Johnson, your heart's not beating. It was erratic from the tests, and you have to go now. The staff will be awaiting your arrival."

My sister provided transportation for me, and all the while, I was realizing I was dying. I arrived at the emergency room, and the surgical staff were there, waiting. I was consulted and prepped, and surgery was performed in less than one hour. When I awakened, they had installed a pacemaker and a defibrillator (another miracle).

Putting God First

Several months passed. My recovery was sure. However, God had not finished what He had started. As I said before, He was getting ready to make His point—and couldn't anyone change that. I grew up in church and was taught to put God first. The Scripture says, "Thou shall not put anyone before me. I am a jealous God."

One glorious Sunday my pastor's sermon was about Job. In addition, he spoke about how God wanted us to be more faithful to Him for all His goodness and mercies. I sat there, taking it all in. I began to wonder if I could be like Job—lose everything and still serve God. In addition, serving God and attending service was discussed. In my defiance, I thought, *That doesn't apply to me. I've been playing basketball for over thirty-five years.* On this night, no one else heard me, but God did. Little did I know that my world was about to be turned upside down and that I would experience events that I could not have ever imagined.

That following week, events started, and my life would be changed forever. All of a sudden, I began to feel fatigued and couldn't keep up with my business. A self-assessed diagnosis rendered that I was overworked and that my body required some rest. As always, I shrugged it off.

Game night had arrived, and I could barely walk across the room. Unbeknownst to me, it was God placing His corrective lesson of the acknowledgment of not placing Him first into operation. I knew something was wrong—but what? Puzzled as I was, He began His revelation to me—that I had placed my personal love before Him, not purposelessly but actually. Basketball has always been spiritual to me. It's been my love for when disappointments came, unexpected losses when I was let down by others, in great triumphs, and that II just loved to play. Besides, I was good at it too.

I went to the doctor and was diagnosed as having atrial fibrillation and congestive heart failure. Ironic for a man who, at my age, could still outrun the average thirty-year-old man. I was told of the seriousness of the tests and that I couldn't play anymore. It was devastation at its best or worst, however you desired to look at it. I asked to be left alone.

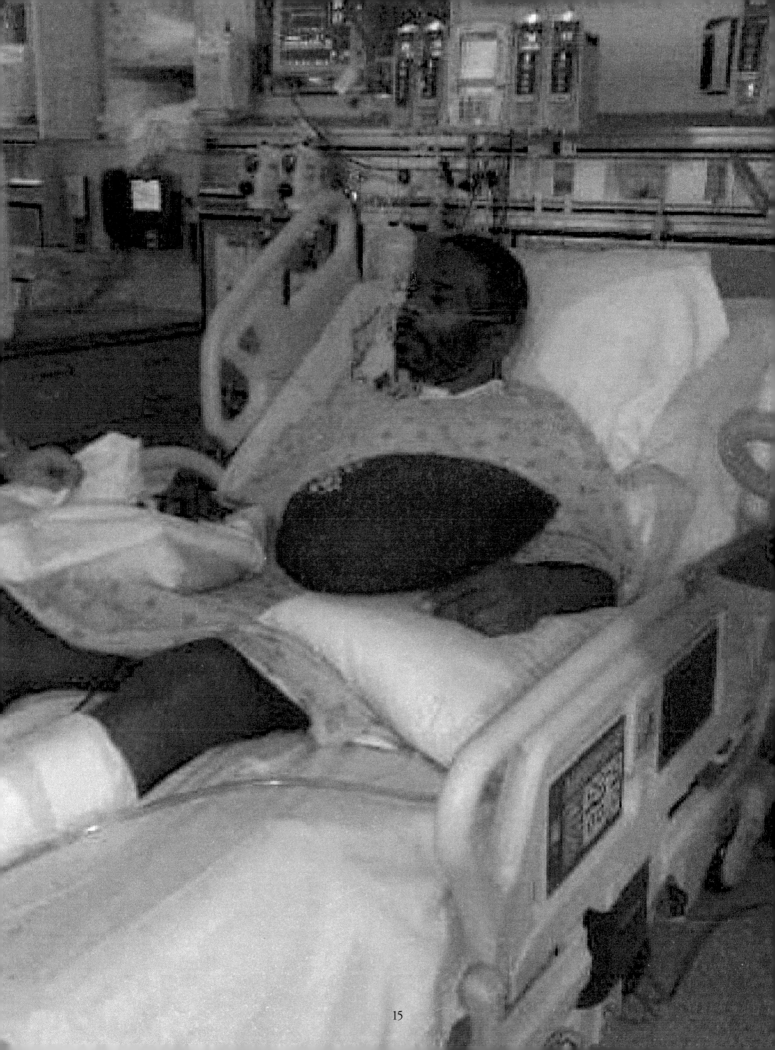

Stripped

During this time, I began to have setbacks in my business, Pacesetter Inc., a business that I had built from the ground up. It included such named clients as Sam's Club, Walmart, La-Z-Boy Furniture, Big Lots, and more, just to name a few—in Houston, Austin, Galveston, and soon to have been San Antonio.

I was well on my way to becoming a millionaire. Pacesetter had been blessed since its inception. All of a sudden, the calls became few, and the orders were less. This was astonishing because the business had been built on our professionalism and a company pledge of providing quality and dependable customer service!

I found out while I was in the hospital for treatment that my employees had taken on a role of making non-approved company decisions. This was not in their contracts. Stealing, not showing up on time, being rude to clients and customers—these were just a few of the negative situations that had become prevalent. Pacesetter soon lost all its business, and I couldn't get it back or maintain anything because of my illness.

New Findings

I began to suffer with more heart-related issues. My shortness of breath had returned. I suffered through a pneumonia crisis time after time, throughout the year—eleven times, to be exact. Normalcy is non-survival after two episodes (another miracle).I was going to my cardiologist frequently and having little success. There were celebrated times of some improvement, only for me to fall back in the same state. Frustration was setting in.

The clinical psychologist told me for the first time that the medicine I was taking wasn't going to make me well, but it was just to maintain me. I was told it was important for me to understand this. Needless to say, I was pissed off. My clinical cardiologist referred me to the cardiologist at Houston Methodist Hospital, and an appointment was eventually made. Time went on, and my situation became more grim.

I had been at home for nearly four months, unable to go anywhere. On the first Sunday in February, I attended church. I was elated to attend because my illness had kept me away for more than six months. The day started out okay, and while I was getting ready, I began to feel sick. I started having shortness of breath and fatigue. I began to encourage myself, saying, *Devil, you are a lie. I'm going.*

Stumbling to the car, I could barely sit up to drive. Halfway sitting up, I made it to church. Sitting there in my vehicle, I tried to gain strength. Eventually getting to the door, I was headed to the first available seat. Several of my parishioners noticed and came to greet me. My pastor preached, and service was dismissed. My deacon friends escorted me to my car and expressed their concern for my safety heading home. I expressed that I could make it, and so I did.

My church is twenty-five miles from my home, and when I had arrived home, I fell across the bed and tried to decide if I was going to the hospital. I had an appointment on Thursday, and I decided to wait until then. It was almost a huge mistake!

Thursday arrived. I could barely stand up and was gasping with every breath. Upon my arrival, the valet put me in a wheelchair and hurried me to the emergency unit. The doctor took an abbreviated look at me and, without hesitation and examination, told them to rush me to the cardiovascular unit.

There, a complete examination was conducted, and I was told, "You're not going home."

My family, along with myself, was astonished.

I inquired, "Why?"

The doctor responded by saying, "Your heart factor is below twenty and getting weaker. If you go, you may not make it there, and if you do, we will probably not see you again."

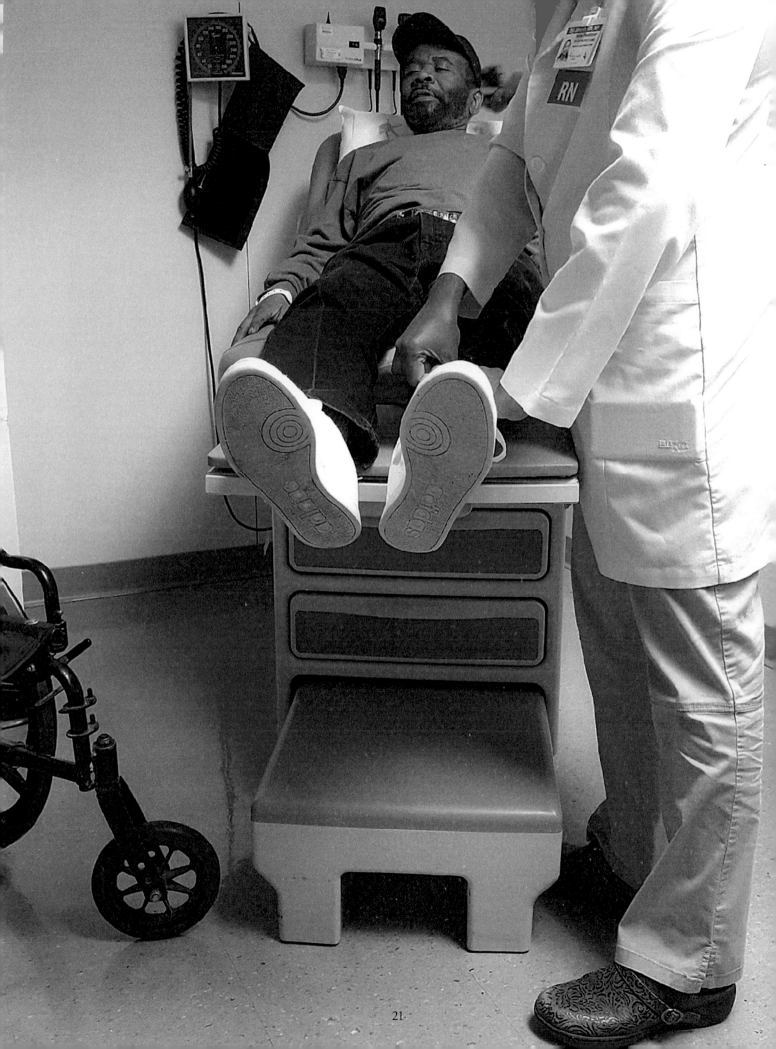

Reality

A valiant effort was made to increase my heart rate—but to no avail. My damaged heart was barely beating. The doctors began to explore surgery to implant a heart pump that would assist my heart. The doctors' further consensus was that the heart pump would not assure a recovery. Surprised at all the events, I became concerned and realized I was in danger of losing my life.

I previously had a pacemaker/defibrillator to aid in my heart's rhythm, and it was never activated, surprising the doctors (another miracle). The alternatives were presented, and the heart pump surgery was scheduled. First, the surgery for the removal of the pacemaker/defibrillator had to be conducted. I was then attached to several life-support machines. My weight had plummeted to 176 pounds, far below the regular 195 pounds I was used to.

As you can imagine, I began to pray because it was apparent that I had entered the danger zone. Blessed that I was Saved, I felt no apprehension about asking God for a blessing. The heart pump surgery was somewhat arduous. An incision was made under my left shoulder, and the pump, with much difficulty, was thrust into my side. The surgery was complete, and I thought that after recovery, I would be on my way home. Little did I know the process of my destined journey had barely begun.

Several days passed. I asked when I was going home. The doctors came in and informed me that I wouldn't be. They had found a spot on my kidneys, and the tests additionally indicated that I had suffered ten undetected strokes. More days passed. My heart factor was still below the danger point and dropping.

The doctors finally told me, "Mr. Johnson, your only remaining option is to have a heart transplant, or you will die! You may never go home again. Your heart is just lying there. In the meantime, we are going to operate on your kidneys to determine if the spot is cancerous or noncancerous."

I was informed that if the spot was cancerous, the transplant could not be performed. Second, if the spot was not cancerous but continued to grow, it would have to be removed, and third, if it stayed the same size, it would not require removal. I, in my infinite wisdom, wasn't thinking about the surgery but about the huge cost. My doctor informed me not to worry about the cost; their job was to save my life. I lay there, wondering, *What else could go wrong?*

While that was taking place, on the administrative side, a personal medical aftercare team had to be recruited and trained before the transplant could be performed. If I ever needed things to fall into place, they did. Speaking of God's timing, the completion of my task force coincided with the positive neurology results of my kidney surgery.

I went through many days of extensive testing, with each organ's function being tested individually and collectively. This is required for the heart transplant eligibility, which you have to pass, or it cannot be performed. I was introduced to eighteen doctors with passcodes for each organ. The dedicated doctors were professional and didn't cut any corners, discussing worst-case scenarios. My spirits seem to drop after each evaluation, though passing. I was left to ponder my fate and wondering if my existence was coming to an end.

One night I realized that my faith was getting tested. If I could walk the walk that I talked, I knew that I could trust God, but He wanted to know if He could trust me. Why? Because He was getting ready to take me to a level and place I had never experienced!

God came to me in the midnight hour and reminded me of a conversation we had had before. "Daryl, you are *Chosen*. This is not about you, but you're going to learn some things. The prayers, cards, and well wishes will be fine. But this is your and my walk alone."

I lay back and let God minister to me as He had not done since my brother passed.

He said, "You Stand because I Stand," after which I fell asleep.

The next few days and nights brought anxiety and triumph. On one or more occasions, the doctors for each area came to discuss their evaluations. For those of you who don't know, Satan will attack you in any way he can. One doctor came by and decided it was a great opportunity to present his pedigree. I couldn't really tell if it was his normality or if it was because he had a new associate doctor with him. I guess he wanted to flaunt his knowledge and skills. It appeared as if he was trying to impress him and me.

After a few minutes of his braggadocios behavior, I spoke up. I said, "You don't know me like that. You only know what's on that chart. Let me explain, I'm from the Big 44. That's Acres Homes, Texas. You can't talk to me like that. We don't play that!

I hate when someone talks to me like I'm stupid, but you're speaking to me like I'm junior stupid, and that can't and won't happen. The God in me led me to inform Him you have the knowledge and skills, but you're just like me, an instrument that God will use to manifest His brilliance. Besides, my God will have the last word."

You have to sometimes let them know who's really large and in charge, and my God is. He left the room, astonished. The Word says that He'll make your enemies your footstools. That very same doctor became my best friend, checking on me even when it wasn't his department's assignment time.

More days passed. The taking of tests and machine monitoring had become monotonous. I was becoming withdrawn more and more. It seemed as though nothing was going right. Family, friends, and parishioners would have encouraging things to say and Bible scriptures to read. However, that didn't seem to be enough. I became concerned about my progress, and more frustration began to set in.

My pastor has always preached, "Your job is to keep believing and praying, and He'll take care of the rest."

God began to speak to me. He honored His word that he would comfort me in the middle of the storm. His assuring words of His grace and promises began to comfort my soul. Time went on. I grudgingly but diligently went through the daily routines. It seemed like every day I was being introduced to more and more doctors. The staff were patient and wonderful, identifying my desolate moments.

Finally, things started to turn around. My care team was established, and my insurance was authorized. The heart transplant team came to consult and explain where we were in the process. I had finally passed the approval of each unit. I was eligible. They started to build my body up for the huge tasks that lay ahead.

Several weeks had passed by. My presence there had been longer than sixty days. The doctors were prepping me to remove my heart pump. After they had successfully done so, I entered into recovery. I was told I would be listed on the national register and that we would hope for the best, "best" meaning it could be some time before I could receive a heart.(it would have to match).You see, I was surrounded by other patients who had been there for more than three years and from all over the world. Many had not seen their homes for that amount of time.

On April 5, 2018, I was prepared for bed by the nurses because by this time, I couldn't do anything for myself, helpless.

Little did I know that my life in an instant was about to change forever. All of a sudden, the door burst open.

The nurses came in, screaming, "Get the phone! Get the phone! Mr. Johnson, don't drink or eat anything."

Astonished by their behavior, I asked the nurse what was going on. They carefully continued to search my room for the phone, all the while not really saying anything. By this time, my phone was found and connected. I picked it up. You see, I wasn't expecting a call of any kind or from anyone.

The voice on the other side said, "Mr. Johnson, this is the national hotline for heart transplants, and I'm the national administrator. We have a heart for you."

I was astonished because they had just left my room, covering orders to place me on the transplant lists, wishing me well, and getting me ready for bed. I had been placed on the national transplant registry and had not been informed. I had not been on the list for thirty minutes before I was informed (thirty minutes—another miracle). She explained to me the procedures, told me a little about the heart, and asked me if I would accept. I answered Yes. The financial administrator rushed in with the consent forms. I had no idea they were meaning right now. I began signing the necessary papers, and some of the donor's info was falling off the bed. I grabbed them before they hit the floor and began reading his bio.

The administrator scolded me. "Mr. Johnson, you're not supposed to read that."

I was told that for one year, I could not meet or discuss the donation with the family. It made sense because the donors have to mourn and make the adjustment of losing a loved one. In addition, the realization was that the donated organ would be in someone else's body.

During the time of testing, I had asked God to heal my heart because out of all the things He had blessed me with, my heart was the best thing He had ever given me. He emphatically told me No!. Here I was, pleading sincerely about my plight to God, and He said No. All my life, I had been told, "Ask, and you shall receive." However, God was on a different page.

He said, "I won't heal it because you're getting a new one. That one has been beat up, abused, used, ridiculed, and lied on." God had His plan, and His will was going to be done. God again spoke to me and reiterated the before-known fact: "Daryl, you have to go through this. It's not about you. I Chose You. You're going to learn some things, but I got you. You stand because I stand, and remember—by my stripes, you are healed."

An immediate calmness came over me. It was as the Scripture says—"He will comfort you in the middle of the storm." I began to pray for its operational success, and I asked God for two things. *Lord, let me retain the goodness of my old heart, and let my new one be like David's, after Yours.*

The nurses began to change my gowns and called my family. As they had wheeled me to surgical prepping, the doctors, nurses, and other patients had heard of the miraculous news. They came into the hallways, clapping and wishing me well. My doctors were puzzled at my silence. They didn't realize I needed to be in a consecrated space.

"Mr. Johnson," I was asked, "do we need to call the chaplain or counselors? Are you afraid?"

Did I want to rethink it? I said no. *I got my main man with me. Let's do this.* God had removed any fears, and I knew His will would be done. God had spoken. It was time for him to Show up and Show out.!

Meanwhile, the heart was being transported from Indiana and the doctor from Boston. (another miracle).They arrived approximately at the same time, and it was on to surgery. On April 6 (my father's birthday), they rolled me past my family, who were praying and trying to comfort me.

I simply said, "I'll see you all in a little while."

I could see the amazed looks on their faces. It literally was a little while because a surgery that was supposed to have taken nine -ten hours to complete was finished in five. "The great 'I Am'"—like David, God had prepared me to meet my giant with only my faith in Him. God is good. The doctors and nurses were talking about what they had just experienced. I was on the list for only thirty minutes. The surgeon who was ranked in the top five of the world said "I've performed many of these and I haven't seen anything like this!" My heart was so desecrated when it was removed. It was being described as swollen and bruised, as if someone had taken a stick and beat it up, as God said.

God Showed Up and Showed Out!.

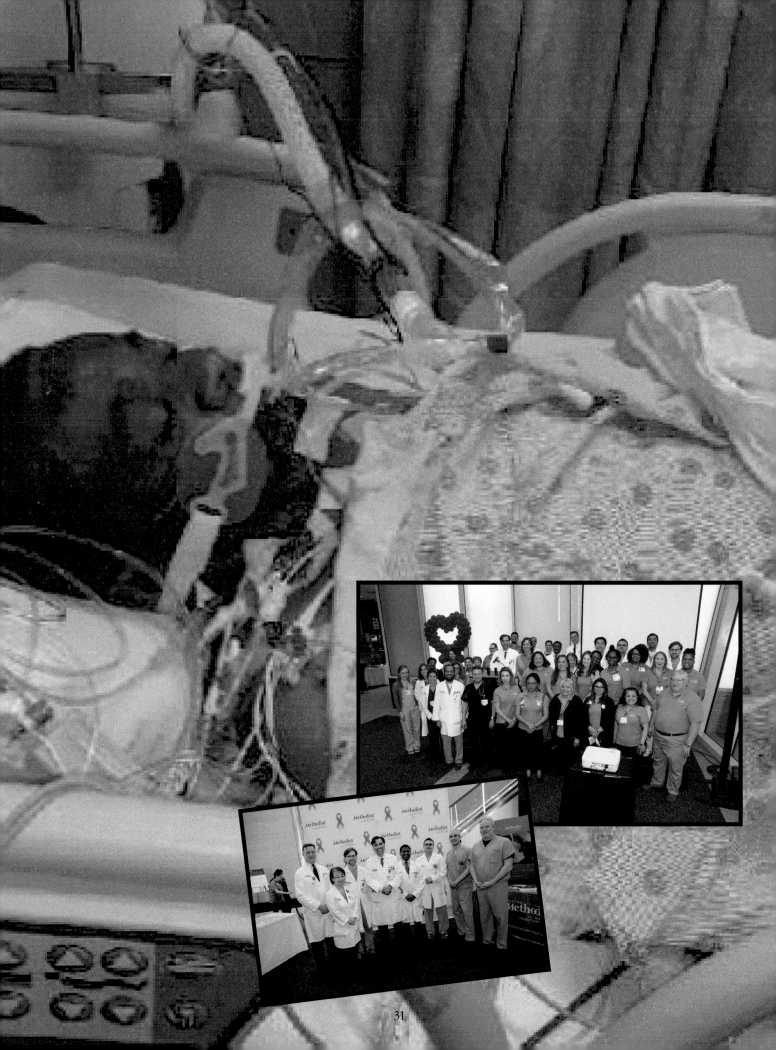

<u>Recovery</u>

The surgery completed. I awoke in the critical care unit (CCU) the next day with my chest feeling like someone had placed a boulder on it and sat down on it. Tubes and machines were everywhere. I couldn't move and could not see my chest. The pain was excruciating at first, but all of a sudden, the pain subsided. The nursing supervisor was amazed that I was awake and started my recovery process.

Later that night, God spoke to me, saying, "Daryl Johnson, Now it is finished."

I praised God, cried, and went to sleep. My pastor came by to see me and pray but had no idea I would be coherent, but there I was, sitting up in bed. He prayed and offered words of encouragement. God is good all the time, and all the time, God is good.

My recovery was progressing well. I began to get visits from the administrators, doctors, and nurses from around the hospital, saying, "We just wanted to come and see the 'miracle man' again."

The circumstances surrounding my surgery were so unbelievable. Normally a quiet man, I was witnessing to all that God was faithful. However, God wasn't through working His will. My assigned physical therapist came to give me therapy, which consisted of several exercises. She had this real tough persona; I guess she had to.

She carried this leather support belt in her hip pocket and would talk positively but in a tough manner.

As she approached my bed, she said, "You're not afraid of me, are you?"

I said no. I proceeded to perform my exercise without assistance, and she was shocked. The next day, I was to walk with restraint, and I did but without their assistance.(another miracle). My teammates, pro basketball friends, and church family came to visit. I watched as the images on their faces were ones of amazement. You see, many of them thought I was going to die, but they had forgotten the main factor, and that was my Lord and Savior.

He said, "Life. I didn't bring you this far to leave you!."

There were some special ones, whom I had counted on for support let me down, but God had a plan. He wanted me to realize that I didn't need anyone else but Him.

They began to ask about my outlook about the surgery, and my response was "God gave the doctors and nurses, the education and skills, Me the fortitude and undying faith, and He took care of 'the blessing.'"

I was moved out of the CCU to the ICU and was monitored constantly. One day I began to tell them about the goodness of God, not like I had ever done before. This was a new experience. One nurse marveled at my view on life, another at my strength and optimism, and yet another about my spirituality. I was even gifted by another because of my testimony for assisting her in her personal life. One other had a praise session in my room,she didn't care if she was on duty. There were others who wanted me to speak with their children and many more to tell of the miracle I had been blessed with. Even the clergy was impressed; they came to minister to me, but I ended up ministering to them.

You see, when God wants to make an impression or statement, it doesn't matter who the recipients are. Once you've been blessed, you have to tell of his blessings. God is good.!

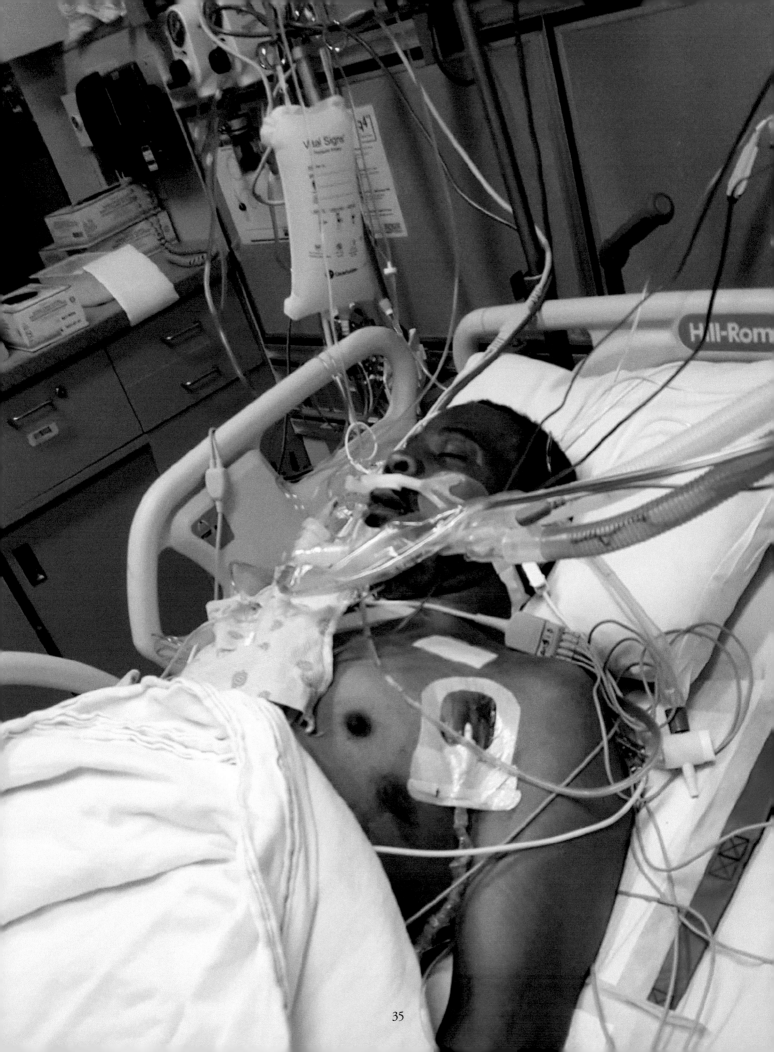

35

Home

More days passed, my miraculous recovery continuing. I was in my sixth month of recovery. Finally, the doctors made the decision that I could go home. The staff came to say goodbye and thank me for being an outstanding patient. They took photos of me and them for personal and professional reasons. I began to look around, and tears started to flow from my eyes, for you see, I was remembering what I had gone through, how merciful God had been. I was grateful and glad to be going home.

It was great to be home. It was a struggle. In my first days, I was weak, and my chest was sore. A realization of what had transpired revealed that God had done something miraculously special in my life. The specialness was that He didn't just spare my life; He also gave me new life—a new heart for a new start. I could tell because my approach to things in life, especially the negative ones, didn't exist anymore. I suppose when you are faced with a life-or-death situation, there's no in-between. Things change. To those of you who are familiar with Satan and his tricks, he decided since he couldn't affect the surgery outcome, he would try to discourage me at home. One day I suddenly became weak, lethargic, and disoriented. A spirit of concern arose, but God reminded me of what He had said—"It is finished." A new concern about my blood sugar had developed. I was taking steroids for my immune system, and they were cutting off my insulin. The result was that if I did not monitor it closely, self-induced diabetes could occur. Satan returned again; this time, it was regarding the medicine. I've never been a medicine person, not even with aspirin, and here I was, taking a large regimented amount. The med count was fifty-five twice daily, mostly for rejections and infections. I became frustrated because I was told I may be taking them for the rest of my life. I commanded that he flee. In addition, I had to have nine minor surgeries to ensure that my recovery stayed on schedule. My progression was imminent, and the reports were better than good. Praise God! Continued progress was being made. However, I was becoming more and more bored. I wanted to do things, go places, experience life again. I began to feel like a prisoner in my own house. It was like I was arrested, confined, just without the bracelet, but God had me, and I knew I was His child.

Praises!

My Testament

Ladies and Gentlemen, my purpose for writing this book was to inspire others, to let them know of God's great love, power, and mercy. When your back is against the wall, even to the point when no answer or escape and no chance of survival is imminent, *God is always there*. He will never leave you or forsake you. When life's situations are at their darkest, He is always there, a presence in your time of need. He wants us to acknowledge Him in our lives, the magnificence of His power, the compassion of His love, and the grace of His saving and healing power. We as Christians are responsible to seek the purpose He has for our lives.

A close friend said, "Daryl, he gave you sixty-plus years to do what you wanted, how you wanted, and who you wanted to do it with." Now it's my time.!

My experience was not a pleasant one. I would not have wished it on my worst enemy. Like Job, I was stripped of all I had possessed. God allowed the devil to disrupt everything in my life, but he couldn't touch my soul. Like David, He blessed me with faith, courage, and love for Him, and like Jesus, my Savior, had said—"Not my will, Father, but Your will be done."

In addition, my experience was so extraordinary. It's not that I was or have been or ever will be the only heart transplant patient. It was how these miraculous events unfolded—the many attempts to correct the heart failure, the removal of blood clots from my kidneys, the eleven chronic cases of pneumonia and blood clots that had already passed through my brain, the four major surgeries in six days and the ten unknown strokes, the times my heart was sporadically beating or not at all, the receiving of my heart in thirty minutes, the age of my donor, and so on.

There were so many miracles throughout this journey. Much of the day-to-day miracles are not mentioned. This journey wasn't just about my heart transplant but also about God's transformation of my life. It's really about my heart-to-heart journey to my life's purpose. It didn't always feel good. However, I realized that out of trillions of people He could have chosen, He chose me. I was to be His representative and voice and be an example of His love, mercy, greatness, and sovereignty. I am honored to hold that position because He doesn't choose everyone, and for that, I am blessed and highly favored.

I have this expression that simply states, "Just when you think." Many times, you think you understand who God is. Then He does something so miraculous, and you realize He's all that and much more. God has taken my life where I would never have imagined. He placed my feet on higher ground, gave me a new talk, a new walk, for He is sovereign, the alpha and the omega. God knows that you can trust Him, but He wants to know if He can trust you. Don't ever doubt God, for He is a way maker. Because of my faith and His mercy, I am still *here.*

It brings to reference when He had told me, "You stand because I stand," and that will always be enough confirmation for me. He promptly gave me the strength of my favorite Bible passage, Psalms 23:4—"Yea, though I walk through the valley of shadow of death, I will fear no evil, for Thou art with me. Thy rod and Thy staff, they comfort me."

In addition, He sent His son to die for us so that we may have an opportunity at everlasting life and the Holy Spirit for support. I realized that God obviously loved me above and beyond what I deserved. I say in my prayers, "God, you must have loved me a lot because you had two people lay down their lives for me—Jesus, your son, and my heart's donor."

Thank you, Lord. "I don't know what the future holds, but I know who holds the future." I've lived to show and tell the world of this story, to honor Him and give Him glory for all He has done. In the words of Marvin Gaye, my favorite singer, "I have tasted success. I've been in love with a dream that will last me a lifetime, of the dreams I have lost, but whatever the costs, the parade isn't passing me by. So if the picture I paint views me as sinner or saint, I won't cry. No, not I. I've cried in the past, but it's easier to laugh about it. I thank God for my wonderful life. I thank God for my wonderful life."

This magnificent journey to my purpose began with Job and his sacrifice, with the heart and courage of David, and the trials and triumphs of Jesus Christ, my savior. I finished my course. I have fought the good fight, and I'm sure that my Father in heaven is well pleased. My life and heart has always been His, and it is definitely now because there is no me without you, for you're the best thing that's ever happened to me.!

I encourage and invite you to make your life & heart God's too. It's his anyway Through hope, faith, and mercy, I'm so addicted, and I'm lost without you. I'm still here.! I've been Blessed Beyond Blessed by the Best."

God's grace is and will always be sufficient."

Amen.!

"Hey, Dr. J, where'd you get them moves?"

APPENDIX

Songs of Inspiration

"Walk On"

"Jesus Promised, He'll Take Care of You"

"God Is My Friend"

"How I Got Over"

"Never Would Have Made It"

"He"

"I'm Lost Without You"

"Addicted Love"

"There Is No Failure"

"The Blood That Gives Me Strength"

"Have You Heard about Jesus? He's the Greatest Friend of All"

Marvin Gaye

The Manhattans

Al Wilson

Gladys Knight and the Pips

APPENDIX

Inspirational Scriptures

Job 1:8

Exodus 24:5

Psalms 23:4

Isaiah 53:5

Luke 22:42

Mark 14:36

Psalms 121

The End

Printed in the United States
By Bookmasters